Children of the Bible

Have you ever WONDERED what the children of the Bible were like, or what they did?

Does it seem like most of the stories in the Bible are about adults, which makes it hard to imagine YOU doing great things for God, cause you think that you are TOO little?

Take a LOOK at these stories and learn how you too can HELP OTHERS in simple ways.

A Bible verse

Joshua 22:5

"Love the Lord your God. Walk in all His ways and obey His commands."

See: Genesis 22 for the full story

I learned to love and obey God with all my heart, just like my dad taught me to. One day God told my dad: "Abraham, climb a mountain and make Me an offering." My dad asked me to come along and help him, and so I did.

I carried the wood and put the rocks together for the altar. I didn't grumble or complain, even though I didn't quite understand why he was doing it. When he went to put me on the altar I didn't fight him or try to run away. My dad and I followed God's instructions and things turned out just fine.

You too can learn to trust and obey your dad and mom.

You can too

One of God's commandment says to "honor your parents". To honor can mean to love, listen and obey with a cheerful and willing heart.

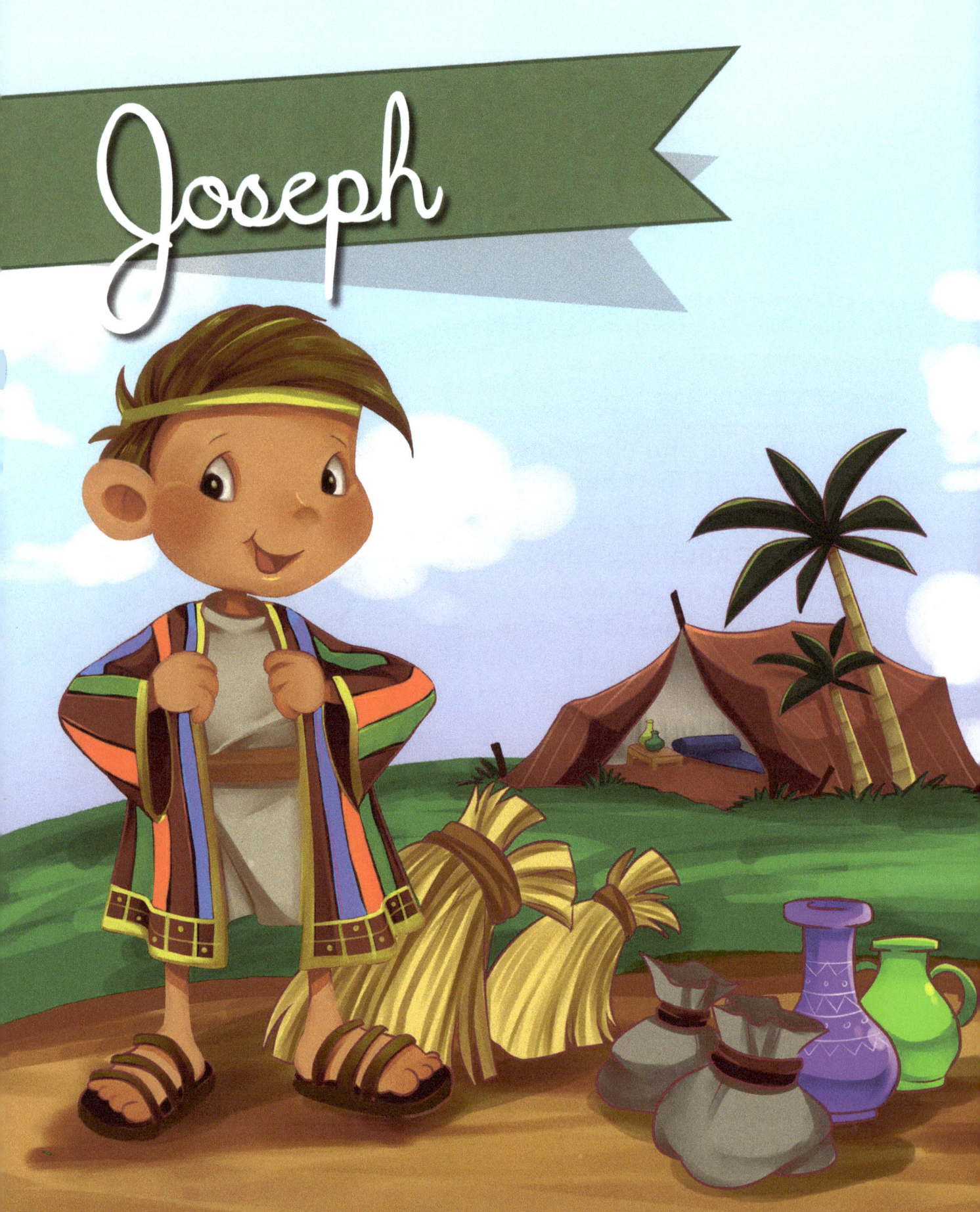

A Bible verse

See: Genesis 39-40 for the full story

Colossians 3:2,3

"Work hard and cheerfully at whatever you do, and do it for the Lord."

Since I was very young, I learned to tidy up my tent and care for the animals, which was a big job. One day, my dad gave me a beautiful coat made with lots of colors.

Then I became a servant in Egypt where I learned how to do many other things.

Later, the ruler of the land gave me a very important job of collecting food for a coming famine. It took a lot of diligence and hard work to take care of so many details. But I had learned how to do a good job and be responsible since I was young so now I could be trusted with more.

You can too

Do you have little jobs to take care of in your room or home? Remembering to put your toys... ...away or helping to clear the table after a meal are examples of things that you can do to practice diligence so that you too can one day do big and important things.

Miriam

A Bible verse

See: Exodus 2:1-8 for the full story

Psalm 23:4

"I will not be afraid for You are close beside me."

When my baby brother Moses was in danger, my mother hid him in a basket on the Nile River. "I'll stay right here to watch him." I said, as I hid behind the tall grass.

As he gently floated down the river I gave him my full attention and didn't let anything distract me. When the princess found him, I offered for my mother to be his nurse. Smart, huh? God used me to keep my little brother safe and sound.

You can too

You can be watchful when crossing a road.

Or when helping to care for a younger brother or sister; you can also help keep them safe and happy. That shows you're growing up.

A Bible verse

See: Exodus 2 for the full story

Romans 12:12

"Be glad for all God is planning for you. Be patient in trouble, and pray always."

I was born into a Hebrew family but when an Egyptian princess found me... "I will take care of you and be your new mommy," she said. And so I grew up in the palace of Egypt.

I had everything that a kid could want. When I grew up, I realized that this was not my real home. However, I was patient and waited for God's time to be with His people once again.

You can too

It can be difficult to wait for a snack to come out of the oven or to sit still during a long drive to the beach.

But what if you baked cookies for only a minute? They would be quite soggy. What if the car trip was over in a minute? You could miss some great scenery. It pays to practice patience.

A Bible verse

See: 1 Samuel 3 for the full story

Romans 10:17

"Faith comes by hearing, and hearing by the word of God."

While sleeping one night, God called for me. At first, I thought it was Priest Eli but no, it was God. "Speak Lord, I am listening," I answered. And He did. From that day on, I never forgot to listen to Him. After all, who wouldn't want to listen to the smartest man ever?

While I played or while I worked in the temple, whenever I woke up and before going to sleep at night, I took time to pray and talk to God.

You are never too young to get quiet and listen to God.

You can too

He can speak in your mind and heart as you think about Him and read the Bible. Some kids even pick a special quiet place to spend time with God as they pray.

A Bible verse

See: 1 Samuel 16, 17 for the full story

Joshua 1:9

"Be strong and courageous. Do not be afraid, for God is with you."

As a shepherd boy, I had to be calm, gentle and diligent with the sheep. "Let me sing you a relaxing song," I'd tell them. But when it was time to jump up, yell, and bravely chase away the wolves or wild animals that tried to sneak up on the sheep, I did that too.

One day, God used me to stand before the giant Goliath. I was tiny compared to this giant. But I also knew that I had a big strong God who would stand with me, and He did.

When you worry or feel afraid, remember that you have a powerful God.

You can too

You can tell Him about your worries, and then trust that He will take care of you because He loves you. What are some of the things that God has done to care for you?

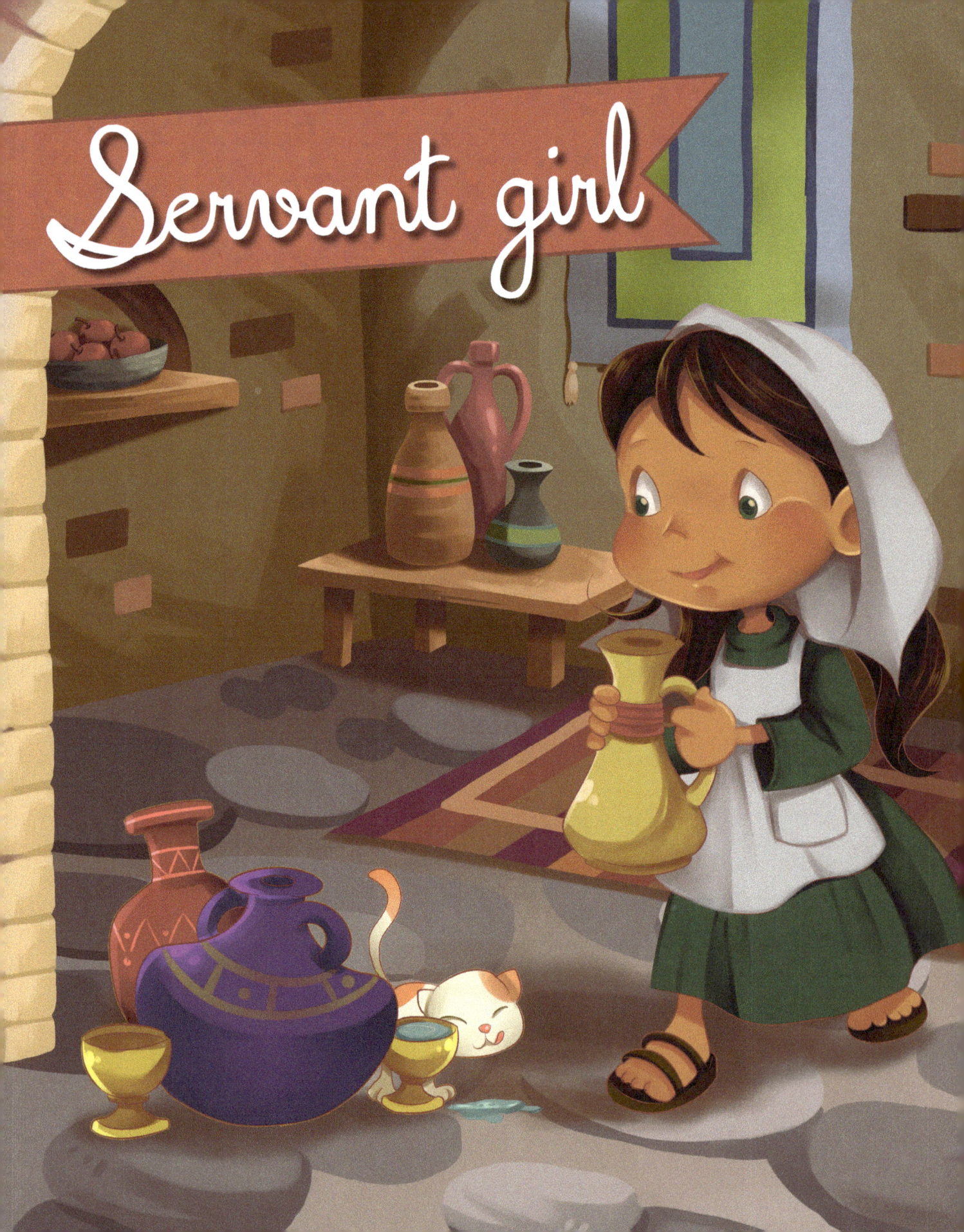

A Bible verse

See: 2 Kings 5 for the full story

Psalm 37:23

"When a man's steps follow the Lord, God is pleased with his ways."

I worked as a servant in the house of a man named Naaman. He had a terrible sickness called leprosy and no doctor or medicine could make him better. "I know someone who can heal you. God can!" I told him. "Elisha, a man of God, will know what to do."

Elisha told Naaman what to do, and he was healed. Not only did Naaman feel healthy again, but now he knew about and believed in God. God was now a part of his life because of the little servant girl who was faithful to be a witness.

You can too

You might have friends at church with whom you sing and read the Bible.

But there are many others you play or go to school with who don't yet know about God. You can share your faith and talk about God or pray with them so they can know Him too.

A Bible verse

See: 2 Kings 11, 12 for the full story

Proverbs 19:20

"Get all the advice and instruction you can, and be wise the rest of your life."

My uncle and aunty took care of me as a baby and kept me safe from the wicked queen who wanted to hurt me. So I grew up in the temple and learned to walk, to talk, and to read and write. But most importantly, I learned to love and honor God.

I was only seven years old when I became the king of Israel. Being a king was a big job for a young boy like me, so my uncle helped me for many years. I learned to pay close attention and grew up being a good king who led people to worship God.

There is always someone younger that is looking up to you, even if you're not a king or a queen.

You can too

You can be a good example by listening to your parents and teachers, and best of all, learning from God's word. In what ways do you show a good example?

A Bible verse

See: Daniel 1, 2 for the full story

Mark 11:24

"Whatever you ask in prayer, believe that you have it, and it will be yours."

On my way home from school... Ding! Dong! The prayer bells sounded. I bowed my head and stopped to pray. One day the army of Babylon conquered our city and took me and my friends to work for the King of Babylon.

I was sad to leave my home and family but no one could take God away from me. I continued to pray three times a day and to thank God even though things were sometimes difficult for me. The king was very impressed and gave me an important job to do.

You can too

It can sometimes be hard to remember to stop and pray, especially when others around you... ...don't do it or when there is no one to remind you. But God wants to be a part of your life and by talking to Him in prayer, you can receive His blessing and help.

A Bible verse

See: Luke 2:40, 51-52 for the full story

Proverbs 3:27

"Whenever you are able to, help others who need help."

When I was a boy I liked to play and sing, to draw and read and do things just like you do. I also spent a good amount of time talking with God, my heavenly Father. But most of the time, do you know what I did? I worked with my earthly father, Joseph.

I helped him in the carpentry shop to build beds, stools, tables or doors. It was hard work! But I could tell Joseph was thankful for my help. And I was happy making someone's job a little easier.

You too can be a help to others. You can use your hands to cook, clean, fix or build.

You can too

You can also help by encouraging, comforting, or giving a hug. Whenever you do things for others, you are being God's special helper.

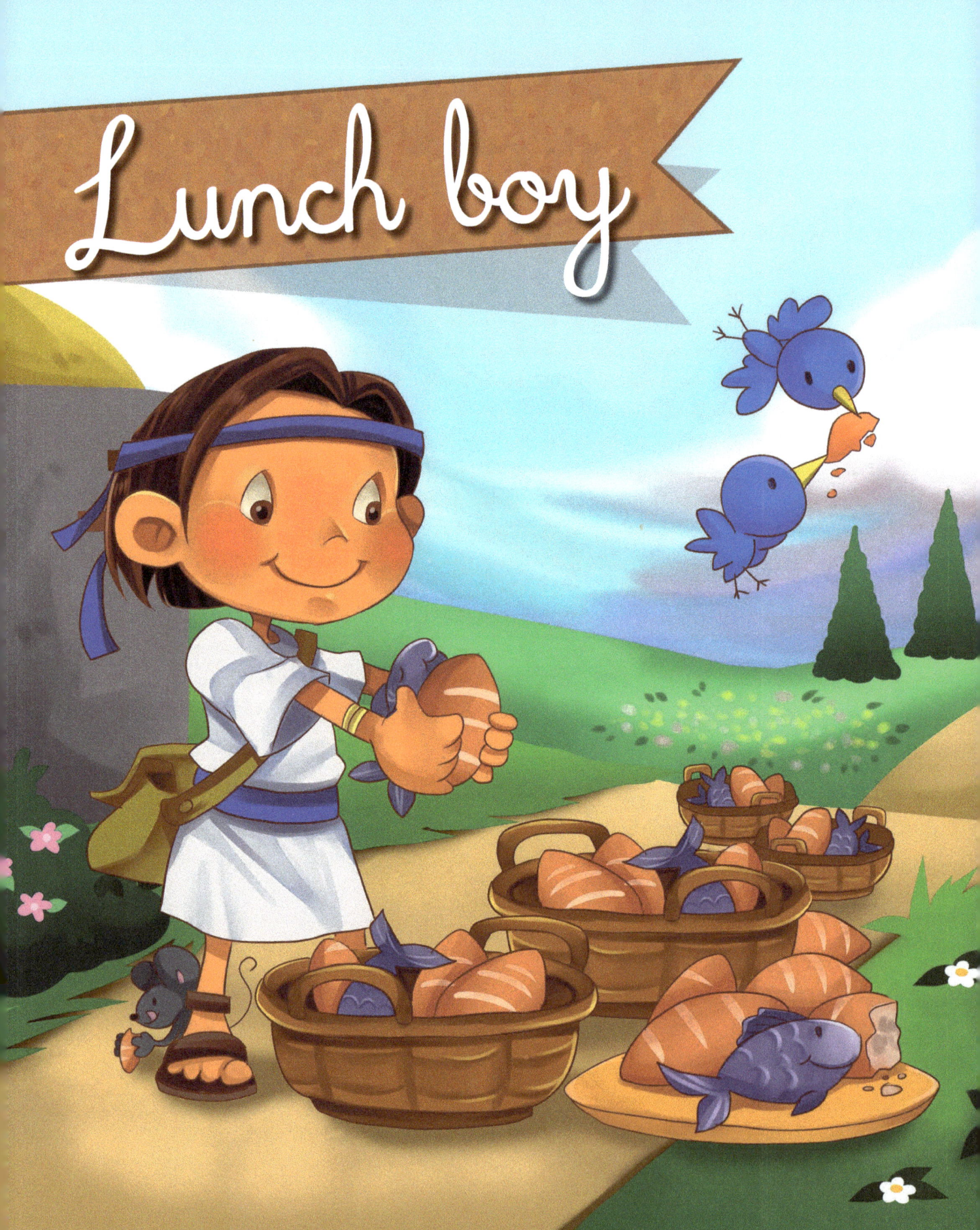

A Bible verse

See: John 6:1-12 for the full story

1 Timothy 6:18

"Do good, be generous and willing to share."

One day, Jesus spoke to a huge crowd of people. When it got late, I began to feel hungry. "I'm glad I brought my food along," I thought to myself. But when I looked around no one else had anything to eat. I only had five pieces of bread and two small fish, but I decided to share and give it to Jesus.

Jesus blessed the food and passed it around. A miracle happened!

There was enough for all the thousands of people to eat until their tummies were full. I only had a little bit, but Jesus made it into a whole lot.

You can too

If you see that others have less than you do, you can give some of your... ...toys or clothes or things that you don't use anymore. Or you can share a snack at school. There are so many ways to give and share with others.

A Bible verse

See: 1 Timothy 4:6-16 for the full story

1 Samuel 12:24

"Serve God faithfully with all your heart."

When I was young, I went to school faithfully every day to learn how to read and write. I also took time to read and study from God's Word to learn more about Him.

Later, when the Apostle Paul asked "Who would like to travel with me and teach others about God?" I was the first one to put up my hand. I had been faithful with the few things I had been taught, and now God was giving me a bigger job, with even more things to learn from the Apostle Paul.

Do you go to school and have homework to do every day?

You can too

If you're faithful with that and practice picking up after yourself, or feeding your pet, then God can give you bigger and more important jobs as you get older.

Which one of these "Children of the Bible" lived in Egypt?

Find these objects in the pictures below.

Find the seven differences.

Find the missing puzzle pieces that fit to the pictures.

Write the numbers in the blanks.

Match the children's faces with their bodies.

Help Miriam find her little baby brother through the maze.

Published by iCharacter Ltd. (Ireland)
www.icharacter.org
By Agnes and Salem de Bezenac
Illustrated by Agnes de Bezenac
Colored by Nadira L.
Copyright 2015. All rights reserved.
ISBN 978-1-62387-946-4

Copyright © 2012 by Agnes and Salem de Bezenac. All rights reserved. No part of this book may be reproduced in any form or by any electronic or mechanical means, including information storage and retrieval systems, without written permission from the publisher or author, except in the case of a reviewer, who may quote brief passages embodied in critical articles or in a review.

www.ingramcontent.com/pod-product-compliance
Lightning Source LLC
LaVergne TN
LVHW070124080526
838200LV00086B/331